Beau —
You have many vowels in your name.
This doesn't hamper your dopeitude.
RQT

SPIKING THE SUCKER PUNCH

BY ROBBIE Q. TELFER

A Write Bloody Book
Long Beach. CA USA

Spiking the Sucker Punch
by Robbie Q. Telfer

Write Bloody Publishing ©2009.
1st printing.
Printed in LONG BEACH, CA USA

Published by Write Bloody Publishing.

Printed in Long Beach, CA USA.

Cover Designed by Joshua Grieve
Author Photo by Gerardo Herrera
Art by Jasper Wong – jasperwong.net
Interior Layout by Lea C. Deschenes
Edited by Derrick Brown, shea M gauer, Saadia Byram, Michael Sarnowski
Proofread by Jennifer Roach
Type set in Helvetica Neue and Bell MT

To contact the author, send an email to writebloody@gmail.com

WRITE BLOODY PUBLISHING
LONG BEACH, CA

For Rick. For Greg.

SPIKING THE SUCKER PUNCH

"I know that men are won over less by the written word than by the spoken word, that every great movement on this earth owes its growth to great orators and not to great writers. . . [The] power which has always started the greatest religious and political avalanches in history rolling has from time immemorial been the magic power of the spoken word, and that alone."

—Adolf Hitler, *Mein Kampf*

"Cool people suck shit."

—Lynda Barry

CLOWNS

There is a dark club full of hyenas
barking at an empty stage.

Jon Lovitz replaced Phil Hartman
on *News Radio* after one night when Andy
Dick fed cocaine to Phil Hartman's recently clean wife,
Brynn Hartman. Phil Hartman
told Brynn Hartman that if she started using again
he would leave her, so Brynn Hartman
shot Phil Hartman and herself in the head.
Years later, Andy
Dick taunted Jon Lovitz about how Andy
Dick caused Phil Hartman's death, so
Jon Lovitz grabbed Andy
Dick by the head and bounced his face off a
comedy club bar.

David Foster Wallace wrote a very simple and
easy to understand book called *Finite Jest.*
Richard Pryor burns. Gilda Radner smolders.
Andy Kaufman writhes on the ground with women.

Bill Hicks never gained mainstream popularity
because he couldn't tell more dick jokes than
jokes about the first Iraq War. Perpetually censored,
Bill Hicks was diagnosed with cancer,
taped a set on David Letterman, told more jokes
about abortion than the battle of the sexes.

David Letterman pulled the segment from the show,
and his friend Bill Hicks died a few months later.

Bill Cosby shot his shotgun mouth with a sleepy rage.
Michael Richards does the same but his pellets are flaccid.
Dave Chapelle walked away from millions of dollars
because he couldn't control WHY the hyenas were barking.

In February 2009, David Letterman aired the censored
Bill Hicks segment and publicly apologized to Bill Hicks'
mother, Mary Hicks. She only half-accepted the apology.

At Kermit the Frog's memorial service,
Miss Piggy had to run away from the podium
at the end of his eulogy. Scooter told the congregation
why we should live in the moment like Kermit did and then
Scooter died of AIDS just two years later. Big Bird
came out to sing "It's Not Easy Bein' Green" and for
a moment it sounded as if there was a human being
living inside of this giant yellow body, for a moment it
sounded like this impossible real person was starting to
crack and cry inside of this now trembling feathered body
all because a frog didn't want to bother people
by going to the hospital in time. Later, the ashes
of someone named Jim Henson were scattered
on a ranch in Santa Fe.

From the stage, you can't see the hyenas but
you can hear them barking. Your job is to be
meat dangling to tease out the barking. Your
job, clown, is to be meat dangling dance for the
canine scream that means that you're winning.

You're a failure if they think they can hear a real
human being shivering and frightened inside
your giant clown body. There's a two-drink
minimum, tip your waitress, you'll be here all night
you say, you'll be here all night sucking out
the cackles daring death to just try and take you.
And that's the joke, you know, life. Life is
a wonderful joke. When Tina Fey was five
years old, she was playing in her front yard,
a man walked up to her and just slashed her
across the face. When Stephen Colbert was
ten, his father and two oldest brothers died
in a plane crash on September 11th, 1974.
Mark Twain tried to swallow an entire planet's
imperialistic, selfish greed, stuff it inside
a funny white suit. Then the daughter of Samuel
Clemens died. Mark Twain kept working,
Samuel Clemens stopped working. We go
on, despite. Despite this, to spite this, in spite,
we go on. It really is a wonderful joke.
It's really quite hilarious.

THE FOAM

The Foam seeped up through the floorboards.
Soon the building would be consumed.
Soon there'd be no need for soons.
The Foam does not own a wristwatch.

Science created the Foam to kill Germans.
The Foam cares nothing for Science!
It will kill Germans eventually
but only because the Foam is relentless.

If the Foam were the subject of a movie about the Foam,
then the poster of that movie would say "The Foam"
in big bleedy letters with "The" written tiny and
"Foam" written in all capitals ("F" actually being the
smallest letter and "M" the largest), and there'd be a
picture of the Foam behind "The Foam" and it would
be absorbing a motorcycle while an attractive woman
screams and a man in a leather jacket attempts to stab
the Foam with a switchblade—but the Foam is not a
movie! The Foam is real, so please be serious.

Police, marines, urban street gangs all try to stop the Foam.
They uselessly fire bullets into the Foam
but it is useless, as was mentioned earlier,
the Foam consumes all into its sudsy maw.

A child playing picks up the Foam,
puts it on his face,
and pretends to be Santa.
The Foam spares him and
he will grow to be President of Everything
in the post-Foam age.
The Foam is only human.

Man prevails over the Foam
thirty years after its conception
and we will all succeed
pretending to be Santa.

ROCK, ROCK, ROCK 'N' ROLL HIGH SCHOOL

Right before I was born—
I went to high school at the top of the Washington Monument.
This was the late 70's—
back when you either understood punk rock instantly
or you didn't—
and scaling the sleek walls of that capital donger every morning
was more than a hassle in a leather jacket.

The pigeon shit up there got thick—
but punk and
high school and
the 70's
were all about moving so fast you couldn't assess
damage or disco or whose *fuck you* was louder—
the state to the world or
you to the state
of the world.
I don't think any of us even had other fingers—
just big hard cocks shooting out the center of pale knuckles—
fuck you fuck you FUCK YOU!

All my teachers were too coked out and harried to mark me late—
being pretty was illegal—
my cold shell was half sweat, half freedom—
we all failed and graduated anyway.

Our smiles were stinking sneers—
we wore our gym clothes in the snow—
obliterating nature with attitude—
Carter left the keys to his dick in his other pants.

For my science project, I punched my buddy in the mouth;
his blood was my book report.
Black and white skeletons
esoteric Luddites
pikes through our pussies, out our screaming faces
electric pomp and
similar circumstance.

1980, I was born.
The partitioned cafeteria persists.

NINE PORTRAITS OF A BAD CROOK

I married her for her money.
Not that she had any; I just wanted hers.
My whole life has been a series of poorly prioritized criminal plots.

I'm a mess
of crossed wires and mixed seagulls.
Pigtails. Mixed wigwams.
I'm like all those cords behind Gary's entertainment center—
he's screwed if he ever moves
I'm screwed
if I ever move.
I'm sorry.
I don't know anyone named Gary.
I'm a pathological liar,
but you know what I mean,
you know.
I'm sorry.
I'm not a pathological liar,
but you know what I mean.
I'm sorry.

Let me be clear—

      I'm just waiting
for permission

to be clear.
O, let me be clear!
Let me be clear, let me be clear.

She convinced me her guts were golden,
her mucous was cocoa,
and our love afforded me a frequent gift
of nose-picked chocolate.
Pieces of her stuck in my big idiot grin—
Oh, baby, it's delicious, thank you.

I made her a fur coat out of real elephant hair.
She said she loved it and wore it once and
I hid from her how many elephants I had to kill
in order to construct an elephant fur coat.
I stashed their enormous corpses in our storage
room, whispered *I'm sorry* into the stinking
dark every night before bed.

I met a very nice Parisian girl in Los Angeles recently.
She said her only experience with Chicago was when
she stayed here for two weeks with an indifferent
Wrigleyville meatbrain.
She said she finally said to him
If you hate me,
just say!
If you want me to go,
just say!
Just say! Just say!
You know, if you hate me, just say.

I told her I wanted to visit Paris sometime.
She said,
Fuck Paris.

Fuck Chicago.

My little feet dangle submerged off the end
of the dock and my ankles resemble mangroves;
but unlike those Amazonian sentries, I have
not yet figured out how to be nourished by water
alone.
My little feet, kissed by fishes, pachydermatic
and impermeable.

Please, lady, let me be clear.
I think my problem is I have a heart.
I have piles of them. I just don't have
a tin man to put them into.

I'm sorry—
Here is some unauthorized clarity:
Our identities are the style by which we procure love.
I thought you were just my style, but
I'm just not who I thought you were anymore.
I'm not who I thought you were.

CHICKENSCRATCH

Do chickens have names for
themselves, and if so, which first came?
Apparently all linguists have favorite parts
of speech. If I were a linguist, my favorite part
of speech would be the pronoun. I am not
a linguist. I am—among other things—a poet
who is supposed to minimize pro
nouns, not encourage them whose
name—for that matter—is a verb that means
to steal, but then there's all the editing one does
by using pronouns:
I am a we with some of them and most
of me, and even if chickens don't have names
I bet they have pronouns:
she-cluck
I-ba-guck
we-cock-
a-doodle-
doo, and
can there be shwes and hwes and thmes?
Possibility without letters, chickens,
are poems with more breast meat than
brains so
we minimize them,
we encourage them.

BEAR BAITING

In Elizabethan England, a popular leisure activity was "bear baiting," a sport where a live bear with its teeth and claws filed down was presented in a coliseum, one of its legs secured to a stake in the ground. The bear would then be set upon by hunting dogs, with bets taken on the winner. The bears and dogs[1] would tear each other to pieces in front of jubilant onlookers, often amassed by the thousand.

Bear baiting was big business and much beloved by the populace. Theatres of the era, including Shakespeare's Globe, were forced to close on Thursdays to discourage splitting audience[2]. Even still, a Puritanical movement in the English parliament passed a law to outlaw bear baiting on Sundays—not for their horrendous cruelty to the animals, but rather because grandiose recreational activities were to be discouraged on a day supposedly devoted to worship. However, Queen Elizabeth I, a staunch advocate of bear baiting, overruled her Parliament's decision in favor of keeping the baiting arenas open on the Lord's Day. This unprecedented act ensured Elizabeth's immortal notoriety and earned her the additional title "Master Bear Baiter."

---

1   Dogs are the bear's closest biological relative.

2   To the status quo of the era, theatre and bear baiting were nearly interchangeable, two sides of the same amoral coin.

Now try not to judge Elizabeth or our forebears too harshly. It should be noted that in Elizabethan England, bears were plentiful; the Earth, newly round, and nature herself were infinite. So though cruel, it is universally enjoyable to witness the infinite conquered, symbolically and otherwise.

And think of our own descendants—future generations aghast (as you are now) at our attitudes toward water, oil, bananas, the polar ice caps, the Milky Way, and everything else in our world that is deceptively endless.

And think of the forebears of Elizabethan England; surely those Neanderthals passed on some vestigial terror that the eleven-foot-tall cave bears would one day capriciously extract them from their caves and mortal husks with a casual swipe of the paw.

How exhilarating it must have been to see fear destroyed like that.

Perhaps you are one of the very reasonable people; your metric for empathy and morality are perfectly calibrated so that right and wrong always sit on opposite sides of your mind, like boys and girls at an eighth grade dance. But entertain with me for a moment that you are not so reasonable; pretend that you're one of the evil boys; after all, a version of yourself, an analogue of who you are in this society—teacher, doctor, artist—sat in the bear baiting bleachers and let the spectacle fill them with joy. They were a community, anonymous as a theatre audience, boys and girls, laughter and cheers, dancing together.

Clearly, this is why bears in mainstream family culture vacillate between the humorous and the adorable—it is just a modern display of baiting. With every laugh these pages herein[3], every teddy bear clutched comfortingly close, every polar bear hawking Coca Cola, every Berenstein Bear exploit and foible, another mallet strike drives the stake down.

"Watch the big scary bear, Abigail. Isn't he dreadful? Watch him go down. He'll pay for being so dreadful."

However, besides commonplace huggable simulacra, the literal practice of bear baiting still goes on today in parts of Pakistan. Apparently they did not get the animal rights memo. Indeed, the impoverished masses of the third world are excessively challenged in the memo-getting department. They are still burdened with an authentic reality and its non-metonymic daily struggles. Burdened with real deserts[4]. Burdened with a real Mother Nature, with real teeth and claws who at any moment may capriciously remove them with a casual swipe of the paw.

---

3   There are at least five pieces regarding bears in this book, after all.

4   Not the desert of the real. Not the theatre. Not this desert theatre.

TEPID EYE MOVEMENT

I tried to make popcorn in my glass coffeepot on its hotplate.
It looked right but I'd cooked it just past its melting point.

Usually my anxiety balls itself up into spheres on its own,
rolls simply out of my ears onto the floor. When it's windy

or I'm sleeping, it turns into a long thin wisp and snares me
into all manner of drama. Someday I hope to collect these strands

of fear on a Q-Tip paper tube like cotton swab candy and serve it
to the carnival kids so they'd cease incessant scream-crying,

or I'd self-swallow the gray cloud and await my lightning
nipples clap gasses rainy leakage cruel rebirth feces even

though it all came from my head initially, there's no way
I'm stuffing that shit back in there now. Every day meticulous

furnishing and grocery shopping brings me closer to some
thing always messes it up by the 2nd or 3rd REM cycle, so

it seems. That's what it do, it seems, so that my things end up
and overturned in the dream's terrible stain every morning.

I gotta go back to the store house door mouse harmless harness
power strip day trip sticky pick deer tick fake sick sugar shits

what is that—Arabic? Restock, wake up, restock, wake up,
shake down the lines, shake down the lines, shake down.

CHICAGO PUBLIC SCULPTURE #1: THE BEAN

Twelve seagulls sit atop you
as if they collectively decided
to lay this magic reflective misshapen
egg. This is unconfirmed, though they
have definitely decided collectively to
poop on you. This is confirmed.

Inside there must be plutonium bars.
There must be dodo babies and
dinosaurs of meat.
There must be all those lost mixtapes and
the previously clean moldy pictures I
just threw away.
Spider webs of hypothetical alternate
histories with all my lost
twitching flies in the silk.
This is unconfirmed.
This is where new ways of expressing frailty
live. This is where new waves of possibility live this
life error-free and soaked in redemption.

Understand when I say God
I mean "holy shit!"
When I say magic bean
I mean "God."
I, mean God, dink a giant ball-peen hammer

hatch the mirror maybe full of bone and
muscle maybe full of something, maybe full of giant
    seagull
baby, maybe full of nothing, see yourself
in shell pick up shards Windex the poop with a triple
    squeak
see yourself in my God, no matter what, you
see yourself full of protein and decline,
the point is
SMASH
whatever's in there hasn't an egg tooth,
hasn't a phone booth, the point is
SMASH, mean God
SMASH
SMASH
SMASH yourself free.

DEAR FLUFFY WALRUS,

I regret to tell you
my wife and I no longer require
your sooth-saying services.
Please dislodge yourself from our bath
and replace all the shampoo you've used—
that was never included.
I do not care if your bouncy curls
aide in your clairvoyance.
I do not care about you anymore,
Fluffy Walrus.

I hope your temperament will contain
largesse on par with your largeness
and you will not predict misfortune for us
out of malevolence, bruised feelings,
or that famous and loathsome appetite.

We are a plain pair who
wish to no longer house
your fluffy walrus chicanery.

MENTAL GRAFFITI: ANOTHER CHICAGO POEM

Chicago, when will you be angelic?
When will you realize the graffiti is a gift?
Perhaps when we realize that the hyper segregation you
    gave us is a gift, too—
        a shitty one.

You will never be resolved.
Daily
you're defined & defied & defiled, sanctified;
you're revised & reviled & revived, vandalized;
you're revered & despised & derived, redesigned;
you're reworked & reworn & reward, second prize;
you always say that I'm fired before I say I've resigned.
It's a sin when you shine, ecstasy when you die;
through the din you're a joke that is dirty & divine.
I miss you when I'm gone but ne'er do I pine,
because no one pines anymore
and it's not your style,
with all your scented floor cleaners, car air fresheners,
fake Christmas
trees;
these are the only pines in your design,
naturally unnatural, phallically vaginal, communal in your
    hermitude.
Words made for you hold you up
just as much as concrete and steel do,

like a 3-D dictionary in HD,
    a mutually secret promise
    shared from us in the lispy spitting shush of color.

Shhhh (C)
We give you this gift.
Shhhh (h)
We give you these words.
Shhhh (1)
And I won't pitch a fit cuz you've been painting over our gifts,
if you don't fetch the whip cuz I've been on the South Side
actually talking to black people.

See you in Hell,
Sh(.)cago.

LIKE STARING INTO A FREAKY TIME-MIRROR

My new caveman friend kept trying to rape me.
I didn't hold it against him.
His heart wasn't in it anyway.

Later, I asked him questions as if he were a pet:
Whatcha got there? You chewin' on a bird?
You wanna go walkies?

We shouldn't talk to our friends like pets.

I bought him a sweater and slacks.
I lent him my cologne.
I bought him the new James Taylor covers album.
He shit all over them.

He likes to dance but it always ends poorly—
like a tickle fight or a pillow fight—
someone always scream-laughs-jerks into the TV—
someone always gets sliced across the face by the pillow
    zipper.
He danced the cat into paste.
Dancing is a kind of battle.

He teaches me things about myself.

He beat up that census guy with my flute.

Music is a kind of battle.

I took him to the museum.
I am not cruel.
He tried to use the display animals like household
    appliances.
He slid down the tail of the Apatosaurus skeleton.
His toes sounded like a piano when he bowled.

I'm just kidding.
We didn't go to the museum.

DOUCHEBAG, *OR*
PSEUDO-FEMINIST HIPPIE DOUCHEBAG

A douche is a jet of water or chemicals
that a woman may shoot into her vagina
for many reasons.
Generally unhealthy,
douches destroy useful bacteria
that aid in the natural maintenance
of the vagina, leading to infection and
not significantly preventing pregnancy or
the spread of STDs.

A bag is a container of flexible material
with an opening at the top used for carrying things
like dream catchers,
like hookahs,
like pieces of shit
like you,
like you, sir, are a douchebag,
and I would like to be violent at you.

I see you back there
stalking the halls of women's
studies programs and the Whole
Foods olive bar just waiting
for the opportunity to bring up
What Would Gaia Do in a conversation,

just waiting for someone to notice
your 100% organic, free trade yoga ball.
Yes, douchebag, we are all impressed
by your mud chivalry.

Please,
please tell me about my aura.
Please tell me to be cool, man.
Please tell me about how many
misogynistic paper towel companies
you're currently boycotting.
Make sure you say it loud enough
for the ladies to hear.
Oh, please.

Hey—loosen up! You'd be more receptive to this back rub if you opened your chakras!

Heeeey—I read that science and stuff has successfully generated sperm cells from bone, potentially making dudes obsolete! Can I touch your boob?

Hey—I hate men. Wanna give me a blow-j?

You're not even trying anymore, douchebag!

I would like to talk about actual douches once more—
they are not new.
At the turn of the last century, some douches required
women to add a little bit of the liquid metal mercury into them

all in the fight against not-so-freshness.
My great-great aunt, Elsie Belle Wolling McCormac,
along with thousands of other shame-stalked women,
incorrectly measured the mercury
in her douche and died an excruciating death
as the metal obliterated her womb.

Do you know about control?
Can you see the connection at all?
There's a warning label on the box
but I don't think it's long enough for you.
The wicked tendrils of your soft
persuasion tearing at the wall
paper of someone else's room, you
pick-pocket, snake oil freighter,
fox in feathers waltzing freely
about the chicken coop.

Often a woman will employ the services
of a douche in order to cleanse herself
of blood, odor, semen. As it turns out,
the best way to accomplish this cleansing
is to let the vagina's unique microbial environment
do this work
itself.

To the perpetuators of shame, supplication,
and bacterial vaginosis, please,
give yourselves a shower, and let the vagina clean itself.
Just let it clean itself.

OBJET D'BEATDOWN

The most dangerous objects at my fingertips
are:
   a small tea pot and saucer and tea cup
     filled with hibiscus-scalding potential,
   an unlit dining candle,
   a decorative gourd,
   and an orange 36-ounce refillable water bottle
     full of
          water
   and bludgeoning
     (should the combat turn hand-to-hand).

Of course I hope that the war(s)
doesn't/on't reach my coffeeshop
but should they come,
I'm ready. . .

Ding!
My gourd would be thrown first—well-shy of the
    intruder's own—
this'd be so he'd underestimate me.
Don't bring a tumor-ridden decorative inedible tchochke-fruit to
    a gunfight...
    he'd begin to think,
but around the third adjective the shattered pot searing
    tea cup and saucer frisbee discus'll make him WISH he

were merely hypothetical—blind and crying,
the salty lachrymations about his face all sting-y and burn-
    y and melty-y'd
motivate thrashings as a salmon'd in my teeth (I'm a bear,
    I'm a bear now).
Bulging confident I'd ignite my candle, let it melt a
    mouthful of wax,
saunter to,
then mount, my
giant man-salmon
and pour silent his Barbaric yelping.
Bucked about I'd bring my orange bludgeon fury down
    two-handed, two-handed,
like a face-mashing machine until the job is done, two-
    handed, a machine.
I'd scoop up his weepy waxy penultimate oxygenated
    bloods and finger paint symbols on my bear/bare chest
    (I'm shirtless now; barely hairy)
figures like "Anarchy" and "That Thing Prince Used to
    Use for His Name" and
"A Freaky Lobster."
AAEeeEEeeEYYAHHhhCHhhCHHhhGrrRrrRRgghHH*hack!*
The seven other people in here currently'd all be convinced
    of their own courage and deadliness and we'd scurry
    out—shirtless and be-symbol'd and screaming
  Umbrellas
  Laptops
  And tip jars aloft
between our brains and brays
we'D be

rEady to annihilate eVil,
recruit the gOod,
sUpport the tRoops,
do something with these hands, these hands,
give them a righteous memory, these hands.
I'm ready/already a machine.

ITALICS MINE

The workers emerge wide-eyed,
open-palmed,
forward-leaning,
heart-emphasizing,
emphysema-euphemisms,
out
the dust cloud.
They stride
confidence.
Only families blessed with caution
lose love in lightless holes.
Only brash survivors file suit.
Only their bold blood return from under
mine (bold **re-
turn**) author-
ity (under-
line <u>authority</u>.)
Everyone knows that.
Get it?
I
  never
    loved
      you.
Clearly freaking God.
Lights Up.

Stress the stress.
Dust settles.

THE IGGY POP HORROR SHOW

The main character
in this slasher flick,
he's no heroine.
Too beautiful and addled,
too slutty experienced to spare.

Every night he's murdered
invisibly while the Stooges
amplify baby death rattles,
the crowd scream-laughing
as he gets what he deserves.
Final Girl, speedy shell-less
turtle, unstoppable meaty steel
in a peanut brittle world.

Prepping for the horror,
he shoots up gallons of blood
to refill his chest's armored tank,
to splatter and awe,
to open the spigot an'
let the motherfuckers drown.

MY ANUS HAS A BUCKTOOTHED GARDEN

whose sole crop is the assassination of rabbits.
I discovered this while unwittingly weeding.

How disappointing it was when we
discovered but three to five universes occupying
our organs at any given time. When we
were high back in '76 seemed like it had
to be at least maybe a billion maybe a
billion and six not even as if in fact—

I find the prospect of sleeping with you
nauseating; someone, please, anyone, please
make me vomit with this spoon, choke me
with this spoon, this one, this spoon here, right
here.
      Yeah
      Yeah yo
      Yo yo uh
      You be like
            I'm all up on this, Jack
            I'll reverse yo' peristalsis
            Like my name wuz Ipecac
            What!

Accidental alchemy will be the salvation
of the race. QUICK! You shave with this

blow torch. You invent zygote billiards. You
lynch muffins—everybody: DIG!
Follow the rabbit where it did and didn't
go.

Did you see that sad sedated Reese's
macaque in the back of National Geographic?
He'd cry indigestible emetic peanut butter
tears if he had but full consciousness.
Avoid his bush meat glare and leave
him within his brown-ridged wrapping
and do not develop a quirky method for
his ingestion break his nose and fire him
into restrained space and he'll return a
hero and he'll write historical fan fiction
that'll always end before the tragic end.
Thank you, Monk, and take any rabbit you
like.

UNDERGROUND RAILROAD

Perhaps the subway is why
you now find the underground railroad
so mundane.

The compassionate suicidal bravery of a
few 19th-century saints
is assuredly obscured behind Jared and
his big ol' clown pants.

Harriet's gotta amp up her marketing—
especially with the rise of quizno's,
chipotle, schlotzsky's, et cetera. . . .
I don't think she even has a sneeze
guard.

And "*Tub*man"? (gross)
can hardly compete with an
army of 6" subs w/ 6 grams of fat
or less!

Her long impossible blood-strides
surely more costly than five dollars apiece.
What a deal!

I try to change her name to "Harriet Sveltelady" on
Wikipedia, but they keep changing it back.
Racists.

The oncoming crush of roaring humanity's
growling tumblies
drowns out my half-heart bullhorn, and
I'll eventually have to board, too, or
else surely starve—or worse:
be a fatty tub-man.

We must eat to lose, y'all.
We must eat.
We must lose.

*for more info, visit subway.com.

AWKWARD SCARS

Do you see this one?
Got it from a sniper perched up by D'nang.
See these?
Sharks—thousands of sharks. They came after me because
    I told 'em they were ugly sharks.
This one's the shape of a lady.
I got it from kissing the devil in the manner of the French.
    The devil dared me to and Pappy done told me: *Boy,*
    you always take on the devil's dares—it's how you prove to
    God you ain't a faggot!

I don't have a Pappy who done tells me things…

Obviously
our scars,
like accidental tattoos,
carry stories
that we tell
whenever prompted
and because of the storyteller and
their personal brushes with
varying degrees of danger
each scar will inevitably reflect
their keeper's personality.

I knew a kid in high school
who was cut across the stomach
by a bear while he was sleeping in a tent—

he knew this made him a badass
and he acted like one, too.

Patrick
has a keloid scar where they put in
one of those big metal bars
through the cartilage in his ear
because he asked to have that done to him
on purpose.

Annie
has a shimmering gash on her forearm
from when she fell into irony
trying to play a prank
on her little sister.

Each scar-bearer—badass, masochist, prankster—
has their stock stories
they unfurl
each time inquired about these
individual imperfections. They
are shamans of their skin, the
storytellers of their flesh, walking
reminders of the pain their identity's
culture has endured.

Now I present for your consideration
my real scars.
See if you can figure out who I am:

See:
On my left hand,

a tiny slit from fourth grade 4-H carving class.
My first and last 4-H carving class.
I was trying to make a cowboy hat
out of balsa wood and kept slipping,
kept cutting my hand.
This scar is from when I was too
embarrassed to ask for another band-aid
because after my third
they began making fun of me.

See:
Inside my right hand,
a piece of pencil lead.
It broke off when I jerked
my hand away from my
first and last 6th grade friend
because he was trying to
wipe his boogie on me.

See:
About my face, chest, arms,
chicken pox craters.
I started getting the little poxes
on vacation in Orlando,
my first and last,
and I thought they were zits
so I kept aggressively
popping
them.

See:
The back of my head,
the roof of a bank
blew off and landed on me
in the passenger seat of a Chevy Suburban.
If I hadn't been slouching
I would have had my skull crushed.
It was the first and last time
I've driven in a tornado watch.
It was also the first and last time
a fucking bank landed on my head.

See:
The bottom of my right foot,
I stepped on a piece of glass
while running barefoot in the snow
for the first and last time.
That was the joke!
Run barefoot in the snow!
I'm a fucking idiot!

See:
My right shin,
I fell—slipped in wet paint
playing
paintball
for the first and
second-to-last time—
I had to go back,
to make sure paintball

was just absolutely horrible.
Turns out it is.

That's all of them.
All my inescapable stories.
You probably have a good idea
who I am now, but
in those six little stories I've told
a thousand times
they've been edited
to fit tiny narrative arcs,
bite-size stanzas,
so I can get through them,
so I can represent just who I think I am,
so I can pretend to control this pile of fear
I call Robbie Q. Telfer.

But these aren't the stories
I want to carry on my body.
They're not even the whole picture.

See:
(Left hand) Carving class, never finishes or masters anything.
(Right palm) Pencil lead, no genuine friendships.
(Face, chest, arms) Chicken pox, always making things worse.
(Back of head) Roof of bank, the sport of the Gods.
(Bottom of foot) Broken glass, fucking stupid.
(Right shin)
    I didn't get the scar from paintball.
    I got it from the doctors

who cut my leg open and drained it
for an hour and a half
because I never healed from the paintball fall
internally.
And I was awake the whole operation
and I was holding my mother's hand
crying while Greg, my stepdad, cracked jokes
in the corner to keep me conscious.

See:
(Left hand) Perpetual amateur.
(Right palm) Friendless.
(Face, chest, arms) Dumbass.
(Back of head) Godless.
(Bottom of foot) Dumbass.
(Right shin)
And I know that Patrick and Annie and you
have other scars too
with stories attached
that aren't and can't be
perfectly resolved or publicly shared.

If I could
I'd have excellent scars
received as symbols for love lost
for those lost
that I need to be reminded of,
the impact they've had on my skin
and its expansion into this awkward man,
that the landscape of my body is

exactly what it is
because of them.
I want to be able to say,
Oh, you see this canyon on my back?
That's my grandparents in the ground.
And see where half my face is missing?
That's Rick.
And see where the other half of my face is missing?
That's Greg.
How excellent. How accurate.

Have you seen this nature documentary? It was on again
    recently—where these beluga whales, dozens of 'em,
    get trapped in the arctic ice because winter freezes the
    sea around them before they can get out, so in order to
    survive the season they have to continually surface for
    air just to keep a ten-foot hole in the ice from freezing
    over too and they're surviving off stored blubber,
    constantly looping, dozens of 'em, up and down from
    the surface.

Now waiting at the opening is this polar bear and she can
    see the belugas trapped in their cycle of respiration
    so the entire winter she dives in on top of the whales,
    digging deep into their beautiful white hydrodynamic
    backs with her claws, with her teeth, slicing them
    open, permanently disrupting their perfect smooth
    innocence—scarring them—and occasionally plucking
    them out like albino olives. She can eat a whole whale
    for days.

Grimly she waits there,
and the whales have to keep
coming up for air,
and she's waiting there,
but they have to keep coming up for air.
The bear, she tears their
backs, but they keep coming back to it.

I have to say, watching them die
makes me a little enraged.
I understand why they don't just give up
but only in that way that acceptance becomes
its own kind of understanding.

The ones who survive get to swim away
but not as fast, not without their
hydrodynamic backs
no longer intact.
The bear is fat
from their thinned pack
and scarred ruined backs,
their beautiful, perfect backs.

The story.
The life.
The beluga's back.
Theoretically perfect.

And my scars, my stupid stories—

I'm stuck with them.
The mirror's speakers bleat to me daily:
remember, remember, remember,
they have to keep coming up for air.

For air.

For air,
I'm pressing the delete key,
erasing the tales that fill the holes
where my skin used to be.

See:
(Left hand) This is my grandparents in the ground now.
(Right palm) This is Stacy, my friend.
(Face, chest, arms) This is you, my friend.
(Back of head) This is Rick, my brother.
(Bottom of foot) This is for me, because I am a fucking
    idiot sometimes, and I shouldn't forget that.
(right shin) This is Greg, my other father, half of my face.

Stories are deceptions
but if we tell the right ones,
progress is possible—
I'm only sorry my scars are not excellent.

I promise more awkward accidents.
I promise more loss.
There will be pieces of me
buried and burned,

scraped and scorned,
they're reserved for you,
because winter always comes
and she's up there,
and she's hungry, too.
Counter-intuitively we will keep
returning to her for air
because we know, we remember what
the water feels like
rushing through us
while our symphony of muscles
sings us forward,
hot bullets shot haphazard about
those warm summer seas, the seas
swirling and tickling the cracks and crannies
in our almost perfect skin. We
remember and we
will remember
what that feels like,
and we want it again and again forever and again. Go
back and taunt the bear with your being. Go
back with your backs to her, sing
your underwater stories to her,
you ghosts,
you shamans,
you canaries of the sea,
do it for Pappy!
Return.
Return.
Delete.

Return.
You will *taste* excellent.
Return to her
for the first time,
for the last time.

SONG OF THE OUTLAW GRIZZLY

Certain popular folklore of 19ᵗʰ-century America concerns the phenomena of the Outlaw Grizzly—a grizzly bear so ornery that it'd murder cattle and man alike, consistently evading kill and capture and other human trappings like remorse and compunction (which means remorse—my computer has a thesaurus function). This is the story of the Outlaw Grizzly...

Outlaw Grizzly (Outlaw Grizzly)
Hee-yah!
Outlaw Grizzly (Outlaw Grizzly)

The devil rides into the wind
upon a beast of ancient sin
whose claws are swords
and teeth tear skin.
He calls a nightmare next of kin.

Outlaw Grizzly (Outlaw Grizzly)
Hee-yah!
Outlaw Grizzly (Outlaw Grizzly)

Outlaw Grizz was born of stone
struck by lightning, turned to bone.
His guts are curse words,
his heart's a cough.
He met the Pope and flipped him off.

Outlaw Grizzly (Outlaw Grizzly)
Hee-yah!
Outlaw Grizzly (Outlaw Grizzly)

Outlaw Grizzly hates your mom.
He cheated on his taxes,
stood you up at prom.
Arson, libel, larceny—
he could give two shits, instead gave three.

Outlaw Grizzly,
you don't give a crap about anybody but yourself. You
are what Bugs Bunny would refer to as a "stinker." I
don't think I'm gonna invite you to my birthday party at
the McDonald's Playland anymore. Why you gotta be
tweaking, dawg? I've seen your mugshots at the grizzly
bear post office, where law-abiding bears send letters
to Bear Santa and mail their bear tax forms. You have
names like Wab, Three Toes, and Susie. You are called
Old Ephraim, Old Mose, Old Bigfoot, Old Silverback. You
are old. Apparently. You are Big Foot Wallace and El
Casador. If you don't quit it soon, I'll have to cut you off.

If you can't love yourself, Outlaw Grizzly, how you go
    expect to go and love no one else?

So do not front, don't even play
or else an outlaw'll ruin your day.
Eat your veggies,
don't hit a cop,
roar ro-roar roar, rawr rawr rawr.

Outlaw Grizzly! Hee-yah!

MUCOUS HAMMOCK

Sigourney Weaver told me
that the glowworm sits
in a mucous hammock.
I'm inclined to believe her.

Until that documentary
my experience with the glowworm
was as an adorable anthropomorphic doll
    all ready for beddy
    in a nightshirt-tubesock
        and one of those van Winkle hats.
Also, if this doll were properly strangled
his sleepy face would light up, i.e. glow.

My brother thought this to be an ideal method
for the torture of our younger cousin, Liz.
He told her that Glowworm was Satan,
and all three of us immediately accepted the fact
that Satan could probably make his own face light up and
would do so before arbitrarily kidnapping little girl cousins
so as to torture them for—you know—glowing eternity.

Historically, then, a glowworm has been:

    1. a cave-dwelling carnivore who uses strands of
        dripping mucous silk to catch prey attracted to its
        bioluminescent booty.

2. an adorable doll, catching the wonder of children
    attracted to its battery-operated face-bulb.
3. unmentioned finger puppets based on a cartoon
    inspired by the doll but created to sell the puppets.
4. Satan.
5. that which Sigourney Weaver describes.

But for me, the order happens: 2, 3, 4, then 1 and 5
    simultaneously—

Somewhere Santa
grows his first crappy mustache
while the North Pole melts into the hotter ocean,
    the son of man crowns,
and I consider what to get my sadistic grown brother for
    Christmas.

EFF YOU, OLD MAN

There are many reasons for naked old guys at the gym.
Never as wrinkly where it counts, they're as 3-D
mobile portraits of stacked knackwurst, held together
by the right mixture of fuckitall & whythefucknot,
crack sausage muscle don't quit, bewilderbeest gentlemen
all mange & feckless, a collage of art & science.

Dance on the elliptical, dance aquatic meat tube.
Sweaty old soled so old soul sold sweaty old rolls.
The great chef-artist accursedly deft & delirious.
German & delicious.
    Don't quit;
        sparkle.
It's the
clothes.
    Don't quit;
        sparkle outside.
It's the
clothes.
    Don't quit,
        dance on the elliptical, dance electro-aquatic
        sparkle inside. Sprinkle side, sprinkle down,
        sparkle inside. Sparkle side, sparkle down,
        sprinkle inside. Sprinkle side, sprinkle down—
it's the
clothes that
don't exist—
    don't quit—
    delicious.

WHITE MEN OF MORTALITY VARIOUS

In the dream cafeteria my old postmodernism
professor Dr. B laughs with me about the famous poet
and his secret sexual misadventures with Muppets.
His current students laugh too but ours is knowing
laughter; theirs nervous, supine. Dr. B asks the kids if
they remember my bear poem and one blushes: I forgot
to bring my notes on Telfer. The assigned laughters fall.
Later outside the band practice rooms, an ex-girlfriend
begrudgingly announces the winner of the contest
inspired by the poem I wrote about my car. From the
crowd I yell to ensure she gets the make, model, color
right. Sometimes dreams are fucking easy to interpret.

Stanley Fish gave a lecture at my college and said
that postmodernism was bullshit (I'm paraphrasing)
and the actual Dr. B got on the Q&A mic to defend his
life the best he could. SF also said that if you're not an
expert in something you're basically bullshitting (I'm
not paraphrasing). He challenged everyone there to arm
wrestle his knowledge of John Milton. No one accepted.
Then he put on a striped singlet and spun a Model-T over
his head for an hour.

I wrote comic strip dialogue that goes:

Dumpy Guy: Man, if you don't think ____ is a total
hottie, you'd have to be blind, gay, and dead!

Sarcastic Animal: You'd be John Milton?

My friend said it wasn't a good comic strip because it essentially says *Hey! Look how much I know about John Milton!* He's right but I neglected to tell him that that's ALL I know about John Milton. I'm tired of saying John Milton. Maybe the *New Yorker* would like my comic strip about John Milton. John Milton.

Dr. B admitted once that he'd never read *Hamlet* and that at this point he'd probably not need to. I've read *Hamlet* but I don't have a word for the kind of reading that is saying the sentences in my head but actually thinking about how many girls I could have sex with if I had any game—that's how I read *Hamlet, Song of Myself,* and the first twenty pages of *Paradise Lost* by John Milton.

Harold Bloom discusses Hamlet like an old lover—one who he remembers fondly though briefly as if too much discussion will remind everyone that HB could have prevented the prince's death if he'da just kept his big ol' egghead outta all them books.

I've been accidentally recently publicly racist sexist I don't have a word for prejudice with good intentions.

When I ask the young poets I teach to define Poetry, their definitions widely variate alive polychromatic. They stop smiling and scribble when I tell them my definition. I wish I wrote what they define. I can't believe I corrected Erika when she said *Poetry is survival.*

It's hard to say what I mean when what I mean
is quicksand lightning bugs, I mean neighborhood
fragrances, I mean the birds who live in the airport, I
mean potato diseases and I don't know which ones, I mean
I don't know. I don't know what I mean. I'm basically
bullshitting.

You know?

DEAR FACIAL OILS,

You have a name though it is so ugly so that no one remembers it.
The scientist who first named you was an ugly oily well-
    respected man so no one remembers it—your name.

You are the bounty of our pillows'
nightly attempts to suck the dreams out our ever-aging
    faces, those vampiric fluffy sponges, those murderous
    snuggle clubs. Slumber buckets.

If collected in a small-sized swimming pool, you may
    become quite dangerous to mice and shrews; you
    would drown voles and chipmunks and the baby
    armadillo.
Nessy and Harry would still disregard you no matter the
    swimming pool of you.

(If I lurch backwards fast enough will a transparent mask
    of my lurching face briefly dangle in the air then
    descend upon these here corn muffins?)

You are frequently aphrodisiatic.
Though more often you do not get that credential.
Though more often still you are held in blue rectangles of
    private and minute disgust.
You see you are kissed and you are not what we kiss what
    we see.

The mixing of you with others is like flying the trapeze
    with one's face so that one may aggravate a bubble tea
    whose bubbles have been too consolidated, which is
    difficult and impossible the moment one realizes just
    what one's doing with one's face.

You
are the huggers of fluorescence—the buzzing false tube
    suns the forbidden frustration bats
are not a face
is the denizen of Paris and Funeral Parlors
are the bloods of the Minotaurs
are not good for paintings
are cell phone and subway stolen.

A request:
I ask you, facial oils, that you hire a PR person—
the smear campaigns have succeeded—
for you are not as beautiful in our symbol-ridden organs
    as you are beautiful on you are beautiful let them tell
    them tell them you are beautiful.

Sincerely,
Robbie Q. Telfer

YOU CAN'T SPELL FUTILITY WITHOUT UTILITY

Although he'd sewn sleeves into Earth
he felt more like ass than Atlas
with his arms underground
air-dangling legs like that
it's hard to get a foothold on sky
it's hard to wear your world
when it's constantly wearing you
upside
down.

Can I ask you a question?
Thanks. (That *was* the question.)

He, you, whatever
continues to peddle
on protons
trying for a chunk of real
to be flown by
so he can plant toe
invert heaven cycle
get the blood to vacate
sad strained forehead veins
get down to the business of
economical shrugging
the center of everything
get down to getting

gravity's tugging hugging
his clothes, his skin
worn, lovely, breathless
the center of everything.

In the meanwhile he's missed
the advertising projected
on the full moon's face
though necessity requires
that he piss on his own –
face and necessities –
inadvertent expert he's
destiny's momentum jacket he's
dysfunctional finger worming at
the center of everything.

Who's to say there's a winner
in the war of us vs. the dust?
Thanks. (*That* was the question.)

ELWOOD ELEMENTARY K-8

When the girl is dead
they bifurcate
her prime meridian
resembles dull health
textbook fallopian views.

They pluck from small
intestine crumpled Polaroid
shows the person who
kills her. She takes it
eats it receives murder
the picture develops
in the dying stomach.

Revision in papier-mâché
pipe-cleaner egg carton
casket the cops chalk
her up for each class
she passes she points
that's where I was
that's what was me
papers publish her
honor roll obituary.

CHICAGO PUBLIC SCULPTURE #2: THE PICASSO

Aardvark flattened by circumstance,
you didn't ask to be perfect,
like everything that we love,
there's something unmistakably
fucked up about you and your face.

There's an infamous omelet
that can only be prepared
by cooking eggs on your steel
heated by the sun through
our smog and resentment
legitimate grit stuck in it.
This is called the Chicago Omelet
and it is hard to swallow.

Stringed bagpipe of impossible,
I blow my cheeks blue into you.
There are gifts under your boughs,
there's applause at the end of
your bows, and when the apocalypse
hits, you'll be all that's left standing
of a city full of opinions and lungs.

WWRQTD?

The attention of strangers, the ova;
our poems is sperm
bouncing off her up-boarded boredom
doing our lunatic conspicuous waggle dance
like some kind of high-speed bee
like that fly she heard buzzing
like *bp bp pb* and
when we break through the glass
finally there isn't fear or
Eternity or
the transmutation of a beauty-baby
on the other side
that's when she dies for real this time
shards bury deep in her dry dry womb
while some other immaculate Madonna gets to be
hoodwinked with the seed of our own
deadbeat dadgum goddad
and really, it's all about who
ya know anyway
any way ya know
ya know?

A poerm / spoem / spoerm:

My mouth pupils hack flecks
Sticky pieces of the
Aborted Baby Gee-bus   *bp bp*
Covered in Peanut Butter   *pb*
Reeking of Empire   *bp*

EULOGY FOR TINY STEVEN

Thank you all for coming.
It's really very touching.

Now that Tiny Steven is gone
I am left with so much—
so many lessons and memories,
so many friends,
but of course the biggest thing
I am left with is Tiny Steven's house,
the exact replica of my own
that he and I built together in
my backyard, every aspect identical
to the original, but tiny,
it was all tiny, for Steven.
It was all for Tiny Steven.

I am also left with so much unfinished—
our failed prototype turtle saddles,
the little zip line system from my roof to everywhere,
we were days from completing the mini-space rocket.
Unresolved conversations, plans, and tensions.
I haven't even told the turtles that he's gone yet.
Yes, I am left with a lot.

Tiny Steven talked with me
at great length regarding his
mortality.

Both of us knew he was highly susceptible to
the lightest of nighttime flooding and
eagle attack, not to mention all those
gawkers and their medical experiments,
deluding themselves that the best way
to live one's life is to understand it entirely,
to dissect every tiny wonder invisible.
Basically, this funeral surprises no one,
least of all Tiny Steven.

He told me,
        "Robbie, when I'm gone
        you can give the Tiny Steven
        Ranch to your daughters
        for their dolls to live in."
He told me,
        "Robbie, when I'm gone
        you can distribute my
        ashes evenly among the
        pepper shakers at
        the Golden Nugget."
He told me,
        "Robbie, when I'm gone
        you can use all my shirts
        as beer coozies, returning
        them to their original purpose.
        I'll just want your life to
        return to original purpose."

I'd say,
    "Sweet Tiny Steven,
    I'm sure the girls will
    love the upgrade for
    their Bratz Dolls."
I'd say,
    "Sweet Tiny Steven,
    I will gladly feed you
    piece by sweet piece
    to that lovely mass
    of hobo skilleteers
    at the Golden Nugget."
I'd say,
    "Sweet Tiny Steven,
    I cannot use your shirts
    as beer coozies because
    first of all,
        I believe there is dignity in rapidly warming beer.
    And
        I believe that once a thing exceeds the usefulness
        of its original purpose it cannot ever return to its
        intended mundanity.
    And
        I believe, Sweet Tiny Steven, that I could not
        swallow beer that emerges from a hole where once
        your singing and laughing head sat, where once so
        much life bubbled forth. That would really creep
        me out."
He wouldn't force the issue.
We'd hug and go to bed.

74

Did you know Tiny Steven could do
chin-ups forever?
Something about his tiny physiology, he
could just go up and down for days and days.
I told him we should make a website,
call it, "RegularSizedStevendoeschinupsforever.com."
It'd just be a live feed of him
doing chin-ups forever, eating his
Power Bars and drinking his pomegranate
juice. We'd sell ads, t-shirts, have him
answer live questions to prove it wasn't
a hoax that this regular-sized person
could do chin-ups, up and down, forever.
He said he didn't want to do it for strangers,
that people would find out he was tiny,
then they'd come for him, angry and vindictive
and then they'd start with the medical experiments.
Always with the medical experiments.
I wouldn't force the issue.

I told him that I have recurring dreams
of heaven, since way before I met him,
way before he moved in, way before,
and all that heaven was to me, in my sleep,
was chin-ups forever, honestly. Or sometimes
it was push-ups. Or sometimes it was
an elaborate and endless monkey bar apparatus,
and I would just swing from my arms with ease
forever until I woke up but it was implied

in the dream that it was for forever.

I think we'd both trade our heavens for
our old reality, watching him go up and down
for days was heaven enough. That's why he'd do it
for so long, he was giving me my slumber
heaven. And I'd just laugh and laugh,
laugh and laugh, up and down,
I'd just laugh and laugh. He'd never
get tired. It was incredible. It was implied
that it was for forever. I won't force the issue.

There is a biological imperative in us
to protect the adorable. A cave-person
lives inside me and tells me subconsciously
not to leave cute things alone or they'll die.
When I first met Tiny Steven at that taping
of the *Antiques Road Show*, when he burst naked
out of his little magical sarcophagus backstage,
the caveman woke up inside me, the ancient
communing with the more ancient, and
I immediately hid him from the cameras,
wrapped in my nana's authentic small pox
blanket and took Tiny Steven home with me.
But years pass, and we no longer live in caves
and die in Pharaoh-cursed pyramids. We live in cities,
our problems are modern. I stopped protecting
Steven because he was cute, I protected him
because he was myself, another human, albeit small,
and his survival became my own, sublimated.

Good luck in your Tiny Heaven, Tiny Steven—
may you ride elephants and roller coasters for the first time,
may you have sex with giants,
may you eat a burrito as big as my head,
and while I'm wishing wishes for you,
may you finally be too heavy for something,
may you push through those clouds and come home to me,
may you fall through the sky and come home, Tiny Steven.
I'll leave a tiny light on.

© 2008

stolen from Matt Cook

There's a hole in free space filled with space where some
    space used to be.
I don't mean to insult your intelligence, but this poem is
    about life.
Everywhere children who patiently suckle candy canes are
    rewarded with their first free deadly weapon.
Let your baby become bored with its shit before you teach
    it shame.
I don't mean to insult your sensibilities, but this poem is a
    mentally flattened doody.
These are neither ideas nor songs but somehow I OWN
    THEM, I OWN your hypothetical transgressions, I
    OWN THIS PIECE OF PAPER, PAY ME FOR MY
    PIECE OF PAPER, PAY ME FOR THIS PIECE OF
    PAPER. PAY ME PAY ME PAIM EE. Me own am
    free.
In fact, I fly my Ownership through spacey space-holes,
    and it be long, my Ownership, it be-
    long to me.
Grocery lists are best recited atop mountains and
    namesaked hospitals.
The woman beside me waved goodbye as we ascended
    from LaGuardia and she didn't see that I saw. I won't
    tell you that she crossed herself too, for
the former act is sweeter, more free.

I mean, can you own the wind, the eagle's s(n)(o)(a)ring,
   the waterfall whispering prayers in the lobby of the
   casino?
The aforementioned space was my mouth, though not the
   one I puke with.

UNCLE HOMUNCULUS AND THE TALE OF THE SHIPWRECKED SEAMEN

We're lucky that
the oceans aren't made
of hot sugar glaze—
our sea creatures all'd be so hyper listless sticky.
We're all so lucky that
the oceans aren't filled with conditioner—
our sharks would be so supple
but we'd never see them
coming.
How confused our clouds of coral seed would be
and then we're plagued with millions
of trippy accidental half-coral, half-Miracle Whip babies –
healthier than regular coral, yes
but what of our reefs?
Where will our eels live?
Our crabs will be exposed!
All because you wanted to be
Heart Healthy.
You care about the future
of your heart
and not the future
of your history?
We were all coral once too, ya know—
sifting microbes
building our houses on our ancestors' corpses,

releasing our translucence into the transparent
at the same hour every year
an afterthought
the meaning of existence—
where is the value in that?
Why must responsibility remind us of itself
with every passing cloud and commercial
for white sauces?

Still the sight
of an adolescent cephalopod
makes my uterus itch.
Still the sight.
The growing bubble in my stomach
is at critical mass—
it's gone.

GIRLS PUNCHING BOYS

Inside the arm,
blood vessels rupture,
burst into tiny
future clouds of
bruise, the echoes
of laughter caught
in the solid
moisture, the memory
to disperse like
rain into lawn.

_____

There is a joyful storm
within each of our extremities;
this is the reason for
ghost limbs, this is the
reason for embrace,
the reason for reason,
and the songs our aches
sing to us will be what
the cousins laugh about
at our wakes. The rain
collects. The sun tears down.

WE ARE DEVO

It's like choking politely down the remainder
of brisket after the dinner party's host has just
audibly slapped his wife in the kitchen for
embarrassing him. It's like that, but the dining
room is your identity—the unbearable wreckage
of face. Pretending to be an asshole in high
school was funny but when you weren't looking
these last ten years, you've become a real asshole.
I've been pretending to be a poet for just as long.
Look what the platypus got for all her pretending—
electrocuting shit with her MIND—batting a
thousand with her eye lashes. Throwing all
your spaghetti at the wall to see if enough sticks.

Throwing a toaster down the stairs isn't a
symphony, but it's definitely got a memorable
beat. I know a boy who calls himself Toaster—
what a beautiful tune he'd make in the descent.

CONCRETE JUNGLE

Zoom in, take the picture:

There's a fenced-in field of grass I pass
every day somewhere near the very center
of Chicago.
And despite this field being filled with
cinder blocks, busted bricks, Sarajevo-level debris,
the grass decides to grow here anyway.

Obviously, we're the grass.
Despite the discrimination, segregation, gentrification,
despite the Truth we all go die,
despite the truth that writing about struggle is cliché,
despite all this,
we grow, we live, we write anyway.
Symbolically, we're the grass.
Duh.

But let's talk about the non-
symbolic field for a moment.
The actual grass that sprouts here emerges
un-metaphorically fuzzy,
like the whole thing is out-of-focus,
distinct urban detritus punctuates this fluctuating static
sea of yellow-green.
And that's beautiful.

Not beautiful because only I hold the poetic keys to Beauty.
Not beautiful because Mother Nature is stronger than humanity.
No—sometimes shit is pretty.
Why does everything have to *mean* something?
I love this fuzzy fenced-in field and
I want to turn the poet off when I see it.
It's neat.
I like it.
It makes me smile.
The wind pets it like a dog raised to old age with love.
It waves at me like an almost forgotten
flashbulb memory that I haven't judged yet.

Zoom in, take the picture:
I'm a little kid,
chin on knees,
leaning against a garage now torn down absently
pulling on the limbs of an action figure
peering in at the darkness inside its organless carapace.

Zoom out:
In the twenty years since that snapshot
I've learned to clutch onto all and any
anxiety-free serenity.
I know it's only temporary.
I know the real sadness this field of grass holds and represents.
I know what grows on graves.
I know this.
I don't ever stop to frolic, skip

work or abandon responsibility,
but if you don't occasionally
collect these small soundless images,
meditations of secular reverence,
an invisible nihilistic selfish shell will
grow slow from your inside out
until you completely forget why
man invented cameras in the first place.

Zoom in:
There's a broken red pick-up truck in my mother's
driveway that belongs to a dead man.
Weeds patiently burst from the hood and sun-bleached bed.
Bees dance and zoom out the now quiet engine block.
So much depends on the red pick-up truck beside a torn
    down garage.

I love the dead man. I hate that truck.
I love the weeds, I love the bees, I love the yellow-green grass.
Now you try. Take the picture.

ACKNOWLEDGMENTS

Grateful acknowledgment to the editors of the following journals and anthologies, in which these poems first appeared: cream city review, "Dear Facial Oils," and "White Men of Mortality Various"; *decomP magazinE*, "We Are Devo" and "Like Staring into a Freaky Time-Mirror"; *The Junkyard Ghost Revival* (Write Bloody), "Rock, Rock, Rock 'n' Roll High School," "The Iggy Pop Horror Show," "You Can't Spell Futility without Utility," "Awkward Scars," and "Concrete Jungle," which also appeared in *The Good Things about America* (Write Bloody).

The happening of my poetic life is impossible without Joel Chmara, Mike McGee, Marc Smith, Shanny Jean Maney Magnuson, Shappy Seasholtz, and Derrick Brown.

The happening of this book is impossible without the kind eyes of Karen Finneyfrock, Cristin O'Keefe Aptowicz, and Michael Theune.

My soul is further engorged by Alyscia Bosetti, Ralphie Hardesty, Jen Brody and Shawn Smith, Emily Rose Kahn-Sheahan, Tim Stafford, Dan Sullivan, Molly Meacham, Tristan Silverman, Sarah Morgan, Patrick Carberry, Eric Daley, Joff Ishmael, Stephanie Uzureau, Roy Magnuson.

The spoken worders: Anis Mojgani, Buddy Wakefield, Sonya Renee, Mary Fons, JW Baz, Andi Strickland, Amy David, Billy Lombardo, Kevin Coval, Marty McConnell, Iyeoka Okoawo, Benny the Bearcat, Billy Tuggle, Sharrieff Muhammad, Amanda Torres, Josh Healey, Lamon Manuel, Chinaka Hodge, Brian Ellis, Mindy Nettifee, Amber Rose, Beau Sia, Taylor Mali, Roger Bonair-Agard, Kristiana Colon, Jared Paul, Brooke Lanier, John Davis, Encyclopedia Showers.

The softly speaking worders: Gabriel Gudding, Matthew Guenette, Dan Nester, Patricia Smith, Bill Ayers, Jasper Wong,

Jonathan Messinger, Rob Allen, Lynda Barry, Karyna McGlynn, Dick Prince, Henry Sampson, Erik Daniel, Deb Marsh, Emily Calvo, Laura Berger, Adam "Frosty" Smith, Amanda Klonsky, Bernardine Dohrn, Mark Eleveld, Tom Sweeney, Jill Bonavia, John Shirk, Cameron McGill, Toni Asante Lightfoot, avery r. young, Natasha Tarpley, Bob Boone, Michael Haeflinger, Luis Benavides, Cristina Correa, Justin Dawson, Pete Kahn, Joe Cytrynbaum, the Speech Birds, the Lancers.

Communities: Chicago, Normal, Portland, NYC, Providence, Boston, Toronto, Vancouver, Munich, Honolulu, Seattle, Madison, Detroit, Nebraska, the Bay, Austin, Bellingham, Manch Vegas, Twin Cities, Orlando, Worcester, the Green Mill (and its staff).

My childrens: Susie Swanton, Shadell Jamison, Melanie "George" Decelles, Jamila Woods, Britteney Conner, Lamar Jorden, Rik Vazquez, Emanuel Vinson, Nat Iosbaker, Toaster, Nate Marshall, Ashley Hart, Adam Gottlieb, Jesse Welch, Deja Taylor, Jessica Disu, Esther Ikoro, Cydney Edwards, Erika Dickerson, Demetrius Amparan, Big C, Kevin Harris, L3, Kira McKnight, Kiara Lanier, Kiana Itson, Q-Solar Five, King Keith, Molly Kuhlman, Gerardo Herrera, Adam Levin, Mike Landis, Dominic Giafaglione, Sarah Winters, Alice Thatcher, Raina Sun, Brian Yoo, Chris Kammerer, A Tribe Called West, all LTABers/ YCAers.

Of course Mom, Pa, Marge, Greg. Dan, Vicky and Nova. Keith and Theresa. Keith and Kelly. Andy. Rick. Grandmama and Grandma Dell. Hamrins, Telfers, Postmas, Querios.

ABOUT THE AUTHOR

Robbie Q. Telfer is a touring performance poet, having been a featured performer/reader in hundreds of venues across North America and Germany—most recently with the spoken word productions *The Junkyard Ghost Revival* and *The Tube Sock Promise Tour*. Previous work appears in the *American Book Review*, *Octopus Magazine*, *the cream city review*, and *decomP magazinE*, as well as several spoken word anthologies and DVDs. He was an individual finalist at the National Poetry Slam in 2007 and he co-wrote the video game *Ninjatown DS*. He lives in Chicago where he curates the *Encyclopedia Show*, writes the serialized blog-novel *The Chronicles of Professor Fliggins* (professorisland.com), and is the Director of Performing Arts for Young Chicago Authors (YCA), a not-for-profit that gives creative writing opportunities and mentorship to Chicago teens. His work for YCA is highlighted in two documentaries from Siskel Jacobs Productions (2010) and HBO (2009).

RobbieQTelfer.com.

OTHER GREAT WRITE BLOODY BOOKS

THE GOOD THINGS ABOUT AMERICA
An illustrated, un-cynical look at our American Landscape. Various authors.
Edited by Kevin Staniec and Derrick Brown

JUNKYARD GHOST REVIVAL
with Andrea Gibson, Buddy Wakefield, Anis Mojgani, Derrick Brown, Robbie Q,
Sonya Renee and Cristin O'keefe Aptowicz

THE LAST AMERICAN VALENTINE:
ILLUSTRATED POEMS TO SEDUCE AND DESTROY
24 authors, 12 illustrators team up for a collection of non-sappy love poetry
Edited by Derrick Brown

SOLOMON SPARROWS ELECTRIC WHALE REVIVAL
Poetry Compilation by Buddy Wakefield, Anis Mojgani, Derrick Brown, Dan
Leamen & Mike McGee

THE ELEPHANT ENGINE HIGH DIVE REVIVAL
Anthology

STEVE ABEE, GREAT BALLS OF FLOWERS (2009)
New Poems by Steve Abee

SCANDALABRA
New poetry compilation by Derrick Brown

I LOVE YOU IS BACK
Poetry compilation (2004-2006) by Derrick Brown

BORN IN THE YEAR OF THE BUTTERFLY KNIFE
Poetry anthology, 1994-2004 by Derrick Brown

DON'T SMELL THE FLOSS
New Short Fiction Pieces by Matty Byloos

THE CONSTANT VELOCITY OF TRAINS
New Poems by Lea Deschenes

HEAVY LEAD BIRDSONG
New Poems by Ryler Dustin

UNCONTROLLED EXPERIMENTS IN FREEDOM
New Poems by Brian Ellis

LETTING MYSELF GO
Bizarre God Comedy & Wild Prose by Buzzy Enniss

POLE DANCING TO GOSPEL HYMNS
Poems by Andrea Gibson

CITY OF INSOMNIA
New Poetry by Victor D. Infante

THE LAST TIME AS WE ARE
New poems by Taylor Mali

WHAT IT IS, WHAT IT IS
Graphic Art Prose Concept book by Maust of Cold War Kids and author Paul Maziar

IN SEARCH OF MIDNIGHT: THE MIKE MCGEE HANDBOOK OF AWESOME
New Poems by Mike McGee

ANIMAL BALLISTICS
New Poetry compilation by Sarah Morgan

NO MORE POEMS ABOUT THE MOON
NON-Moon Poems by Michael Roberts

CAST YOUR EYES LIKE RIVERSTONES INTO THE EXQUISITE DARK
New Poems by Danny Sherrard

SPIKING THE SUCKER PUNCH
New poems by Robbie Q. Telfer

LIVE FOR A LIVING
New Poetry compilation by Buddy Wakefield

SOME THEY CAN'T CONTAIN
Classic Poetry compilation by Buddy Wakefield

COCK FIGHTERS, BULL RIDERS, AND OTHER SONS OF BITCHES (2009)
An experimental photographic odyssey by M. Wignall

THE WRONG MAN (2009)
Graphic Novel by Brandon Lyon & Derrick Brown

YOU BELONG EVERYWHERE (2010)
Road memoir and how-to guide for travelling artists

LEARN AND BURN (2010)
poems for the classroom by Tim Stafford. Edited by Derrick Brown

CEREMONY FOR THE CHOKING GHOST (2010)
New poems by Karen Finneyfrock

EVERYTHING IS EVERYTHING (2010)
New Poems by Cristin O'Keefe Aptowicz

MILES OF HALLELUJAH (2010)
New Poems by Rob Ratpack Slim Sturma

WWW.WRITEBLOODY.COM